BRIGHTER DAYS

Vida Theodosia Harris

Tuareg Productions LTD

First Published 2010 by Tuareg Productions Ltd
ISBN   978-0-9549907-5-6

All enquiries should be addressed to Tuareg Productions Ltd, C/O Citycas Ltd, Suite 540, Fifth Floor, Linen Hall, 162-168 Regent Street, London W1B 5TP.
Email: press@tuaregproductions.com
www.tuaregproductions.com
Tel: 0207 692 2711

for

HANNAH MARIE HARRIS

ACKNOWLEDGEMENTS

Twenty-one years is a very significant milestone for me. It's now 21 years following one of the most traumatic occurrences in my life, which compelled me to put together this book. You see, this is the 21st year since the passing of my daughter, Hannah Marie Harris, then only 21 years of age, who lost her life in the Marchioness Disaster on the River Thames in London on 20th August 1989. Fifty-one lives were lost on that fatal night, and my thoughts are also with the other families.

I dedicate this book to the memory of my princess, my love and my star. This dedication extends to my other beloved children in this galaxy of shining stars – Lorna, Kenneth, Christopher, Elaine, Gloria, John, Chip and Andrew – who also bore the pain and loss of their youngest sister. My love goes out to my grand and great grandchildren, who are a great source of joy.

Acknowledgement and thanks are due to my Pastor, The Reverend Canon Christian O Weaver, CBE; my son-in-law, Errol Holder; my friends – Yvette Taylor, Suzete Coke, Eileen Pickwork, Lillieth Miller; and Lullyn Tavares who edited the manuscript.

My motivation to write is inspired by a number of other family and friends, who have through the years read my poems or listened to me reading the verses for special occasions and celebrations. They have encouraged me, and I want to say thanks a million times.

My thoughts are now on my dear friend, Mary Lawrence, a life-long motivator and co-worker who passed on earlier this year. She now rests in peace and the Lord I'm sure will pass on my thanks.

CONTENTS

I was encouraged as I wrote the words of this poem to look beyond my present situation. Hope and determination propelled me to carry on regardless, knowing that God is always faithful to His promises. I was assured that I was not on my own, although at times it felt that way. How wonderful to hear these words as my heart was inspired by the Holy Spirit - "Daughter be of Good Cheer."

There were times in my life when I felt very low in mind, body and spirit. I began to ask the question "Will there be a light in my path, for all around me seems very dark?"

Going in the dark can be very scary but in some miraculous way, God's peace comforts my soul with the words of a song or a poem, which encourages me to carry on.

I can only explain that God's words to me are like stepping-stones across a flowing stream or river, and with each step I take there appears a stone for me to stand on. In the midst of a stream, I can stop to view God's beautiful creation ahead of me. I can see the birds flying across, but I cannot linger. I need to get across, so I cried out "Do you know my lifeboat is always on time." I can relate to Psalm 120:1 - "In my distress I cried unto the Lord, and he heard me."

This poem entitled "Brighter Days" has encouraged me to trust God and be obedient to his teaching. Dare I say this is not easy, for I have failed many times on my journey. I trust that the words of this poem will encourage someone who feels burdened to know that there is someone who cares for them; we can depend upon His promises.

BRIGHTER DAYS

There are brighter days awaiting us
Though dark the nights have been
That mist will clear – so just hold on.
The sun WILL shine again!

I waited long and Christ kept me strong
Through valleys and over the hills
His promises sure and His Words reassure
So trust in the Faithful One.

He was beside me in my mist
And at times I slipped and fell
But true to his Word, the Lord was there
To whisper, "Daughter, be of good cheer".

I mean to go on for His dear sake
And others I must tell
Those brighter days await them, too.
If only the Saviour they knew.

MY INSPIRATION TO WRITE

It was one of those cold frosty winter mornings in 1985, with the trees beautifully adorned with icicles when I travelled from Nottingham to London to visit two of my children. I had also intended to travel on to Brighton the following day to see another of my sons, who had just started University there.

Excitement filled my mind as I looked forward to seeing him. We regularly kept in touch by telephone, though I had many concerns as a mother whose son was a student living away from home for the first time. He was sharing a house with two friends who I did not know. How was he getting on with his studies? Was he eating properly? Not to mention the partying at weekends that I was sure was part of student life.

It was good to see the children in London; we had a wonderful time together. I went shopping on the Saturday afternoon to buy things to take for my son in Brighton the following day. I was now thinking of all the things that students would buy: baked beans, tins of soup, peanut butter, biscuits, tea, coffee and of course I could not leave out my homemade fruit cake.

I boarded the coach from London to Brighton. It was a pleasant journey, and my son was waiting for me at the coach station when I arrived. We greeted and hugged each other. However, he was not very happy about the heavy load I had carried as he took the shopping bags from me. We then made our way to his house, which was in a pleasant neighbourhood near shops and local transport.

It was only when I arrived at his house did I stop to asked myself – Why did I carry this heavy load when I could have got all the shopping I needed for him in Brighton? With so much excitement in looking forward to seeing him, my only thoughts of Brighton were of a seaside resort and tourists. I somehow completely forgot that there would be grocery shops and supermarkets. We have joked about this ever since!

My son introduced me to his friends and they seemed very pleasant as we talked. He showed me around the house, which was very clean and tidy. This was no surprise to me, for even while he was at home he always had everything in its proper place. I thought to myself, thank God student life has not changed him yet.

I went up to his room to have a rest after my journey. I sat on the bed and was giving God thanks for my safe arrival and his provision to me. Just then for some reason I began to reflect on my own life's journey with the children going to all their school open days, sports days and other activities, and how some of them had now left home. I can clearly remember saying: "Lord, you know all about my life".

Suddenly, I felt from my heart God's presence surrounding me. Within were these words clearly given. "My life is an open book before the Lord". This was so real, and instantly there was an urge to write down what was said, and so I did.

My son then entered the room to bring me a cup of tea. He saw me writing, looked at me and asked "Mum are you alright"? With tears in my eyes I said "Yes I am". I shared with him the experience I had just had, and assured him that I was fine. God truly moves in mysterious ways.

MY LIFE

My life is an open book before the Lord.
The pages are there for Him to turn.
The mistakes I make, I'm sure He will correct.
And for the good I've done, the stars He will erect.

So as I go through life's short journey,
One aim in me O Lord, is to count the stars
Which were hard toiled for
And to see you most, dear Lord.

So take my hand and lead me on
With you Dear Lord I will go
Though rough the path, the hills, the snow
The way I am sure you will show.

I thank you Lord for the rough and smooth.
I thank you Lord for pains as well
Because when I put these all together
I sure can say, my God, it is well.

When I first got saved, or in other words, was born again, my life completely took a new direction. I did not fully understand the drastic changes that were taking place. I had a large family that I was dedicated to, I was in full-time employment and I also became a member of the Pilgrim Church in Nottingham. God has kept me through many trials and experiences. My Pastor, The Reverend Canon Christian O Weaver, CBE, has consistently been a great source of encouragement.

I cannot say how I have come through but, with God, we can make it. I am today very grateful for His many mercies and blessings in my life. To see all my children grown to be responsible men and women, and living in different parts of the world. This allows me to travel to see them, to enjoy my grand and great grandchildren, to meet other people, to share my Christian faith and to see the beauty of God's creation.

There were times when I felt alone and been reminded of the comforting words "God sees my life as a well-folded rose, whose centre is in the Lord." This gives me a true feeling of belonging and security. He is the only One who can open this rose. This rose was opened when I accepted Jesus.

I know that however beautiful a rose may be, there are thorns on the branches, so special care should be taken when cutting it otherwise we will get hurt. We too can get hurt in this life, and at times become discouraged. It takes faith, trust, dedication, love, forgiveness and hope to carry on. Knowing that the centre of this rose is in the Lord, I know also that the centre of my life is in the Lord, and I am trusting in His Words. My desire is to make it all the way, and to encourage others on their Christian journey.

MY CHRISTIAN LIFE

My Christian Life is like a well-folded Rose
Whose centre is in the Lord.
This Rose began to open when I first heard the Lord.
It was so tightly folded you see!
But each opening will reveal how much my Saviour cares.
For me, and the pains too, I will feel.

There is real joy in unfolding, and God gives strength
To persevere, so keep near to the stream that flows,
the petals to preserve.
This Rose will keep on opening; the unfolding is in the Lord.
He is the centre, and I am trusting in his Words.

Thank you Lord.

God is the source of my life. I've proved Him to be true for whatever He says, He will do.

I have not always lived up to God's expectations   and there are still many things I do not understand, but I surely know God will always bring me through, if I am obedient to His leading.

He loves me. He guides my feet and held my hands through many uneven roads of life. There were times of greater laughter; times of great sadness and distress; and times when I could not hold back the tears. In those moments there was always that comforting presence, and such assurance of God's love.

These thoughts are a true testimony of how God brought me through some difficult paths in life, even when I was not thinking of Him. I trust that someone will be helped by the words from these verses.

YOU BROUGHT ME THROUGH

You brought me through when I was not thinking of you.
You held my hands and caused me to stand.
You dried my tears when no one else was in sight,
And comforted me throughout the long hours of the night.
Now I could not live apart from you.
I know you will forever see me through.
I love to feel you near.
I thank you for that home you have gone to prepare.

There are many reasons that inspired me to write this poem but the main one is when I think of God's creation. Flowers bring out such beauty in the world that we live in. The pleasure of flowers is enhanced because of the variety of colours, shapes, sizes and fragrances. Let us take time now to admire the flowers while we can, for they're part of God's plan.

I would like to share with you my personal experience as to why it is important to give your flowers before it is too late. I have heard many eulogies, tributes made on behalf of the dead, but in their lifetime no one told them "I love you". I worked for many years as a nurse in a hospital, on a convalescence ward, and it was a great joy to see people recover from their illnesses and return to their homes. Sadly there were those who spent months on the ward, who hardly had any visitors. No one brought them a bunch of flowers, or sent them a 'get well' card while they were alive and able to admire it. Sometimes a patient may have had a bad turn and became very ill. Some lost their memory and did not remember their name or where they were. Sadly, this is the time when people would show up with flowers and fruit. Sometimes that ill person would not have long to live and would have no idea who had come to see them. How sad that we wait for the last moment to tell someone we love them, to show some kindness or to correct them.

As you take time to read these lines, I hope that these words will encourage you to give flowers before it's too late and correct others while they're with you.

GIVE ME MY FLOWERS TODAY

Please give me my flowers today,
don't wait until I am too old and grey,
too feeble to stand; too dim to see,
with my blanket wrapped around my knees and my
zimmer frame beside me,
So please give me my flowers today.

Tell me you love me today.
Show this is in your smile and how you handle me,
let love come from your heart
with warm candle light affection that burns bright
in the darkest night when no one is in sight.
So show that you love me today.

Give me my flowers today,
that I will display them in my very special way,
while I can smell that lovely fragrance
and admire them as well.
My Freesias, Daffodils, Tulips, Red Roses
and Hyacinths, but
for a treat you can put in some Lilies and Carnations as well,
then I can say thank you for caring
and showing your feelings as well.
Speak good of me today,

while I can still hear.
You can call me when I'm gone, Who cares?
Come let's share memories old and new
and talk about the things that attract me to you,
let me hear it now and others hear it too
for who knows when I shall not hear no more.
Tell me now and hide it no more.

Correct me now while I am with you
let's get the matter straight,
you may want to leave it till tomorrow
only that tomorrow may be too late,
then what pain is left in your heart
for the things you should have done
and the words you should have said,
for there is no more correction
in my last setting sun.

So please give me my flowers today
and speak while I can hear,
tell me you love me and show me that you care.
Correct me now while I am with you
don't wait till I am gone.
Share your feelings today,
come let's talk while it is day,
for many hearts are grieved today
for the things they did want to say,
So please give me my flowers today.

Once again while I was in London, my son, John, took me to an exhibition at the Tate   Britain Gallery to see Picasso's paintings. Now, I must be honest, this is not one of the places I would choose to go, but it was great that my son was taking me out, and he has a great love of paintings, as he himself paints very well.

Do you know, I had to make myself look rather interested, but I had no idea about these drawings and could not explain anything about them, although John was excited as he paced up and down. I was asking myself – "what is it about Picasso's paintings that make them so interesting? I could not see the beauty, for I had no understanding of them.

Time came, and we left the Gallery with questions upon questions going through my mind, but I said nothing to John. Then suddenly, this thought came to me, that the true Picasso is in God's hand, and this is what led me to write this poem.

I give thanks to all painters. Long may you all be inspired to use this great skill of your hands.

THE GALLERY

Yes! Me at the Gallery – such a lot to see
The late famous Picasso
What were his paintings saying to me?
With eyes on the walls at the works he had done
But still what were his paintings saying to me?

Such a lot to unfold - only in his heart could
He hold the great legacy of a Genius of the sculptures
And paintings as his life would unfold.
But still what were his paintings saying to me?

No one will ever understand – for the true Picasso
Is in God's hand – for you and for me.
He has His plan.
That's what his paintings were saying to me!

Thank you Lord

I will forever remember how I was moved to write this poem. It was a desperate financial moment and I was ill. The doctor came to see me and he gave me a prescription for some medication, but at the same time I had no money in the house.

I felt really low and so the following day I decided that I must go to the bank. I got myself ready and as I was going down the stairs to put the kettle on, I noticed the brown envelope that had come through the post. I picked it up somewhat reluctantly thinking it was another bill. Then as I walked toward the sink I opened the envelope only to find a cheque for Thirteen Pounds. This was a refund of an over-payment on some previous ill. Do you know, I just burst out in praise to God, for this was for me a time of need; and I have to say our prayers are answered anyway.

I was still giving thanks to God and can remember clearly as I said, "Lord, I cannot repay You for all You have done for me". Then these words came out – "It is all free. The price was paid in full on Calvary. Then I wrote the following poem:

LORD I CANNOT REPAY YOU

There is NO CHARGE. It is all free.
The price is paid in full for you and me.
The question was raised, who will go?
There was a hush. Jesus said, "I will go".
It was with Love that He came from above
To settle that question, who will go?
This took Him to Calvary – Do you know why?
To die on a cross just for you and I.
He paid the price with His dear Life,
To end the strife and win our lives.

So thank you, Lord Jesus, for Calvary
Where the price was paid. It was paid for me.
There is NO CHARGE. You demand from me.
Just to love You, Lord, and work for Thee.
With clean hands and pure heart
My Lord we shall see
That mansion in Heaven, prepared for you and me.
So I thank you, Lord Jesus, because I know this is free.
The price has been paid in full for you and me.

Thank you Lord.

This poem tells of those moments of unstableness, and it is so true that at times we slip and slide, and to put it clearly, at times I do fall. Again, I hear those clear encouraging words echoing in my ears "I will be with you."

I belong to the Pilgrim Church where I feel God's love from the Brethren, leaders and children. Kindness has been shown to me in many different ways, but no one can give that inward peace. There were times when I felt sad, then the words of this poem says so much to me, assuring me that I need not run; I need not hide for I have someone in whom I can confide.

There were times when I struggled with fear and doubt but God's reassuring word and his promises made my heart rejoice; at times I just sing and shout.

This poem offers an invitation to all, for Jesus' arms are ever open as He bids whosoever will to come.

SLIP AND SLIDE

Sometimes I slip, sometimes I slide, and sometimes I even sway
from side to side.
Still, as I go with surety I know that Jesus is near   No strength
with His can be compared.
I need not fear. I need not doubt. His Words have made
my heart stand out. At times I even feel to sing and shout.

I need not run; I need not hide. No! I have someone in whom
I can confide. His Words are true, His
will I must do. He promised all the way "I'll be
with you." Do you know His promises are true? All along he says
"I'll not forsake you". Yet some despise and others wish they could
find somewhere to hide. Sorry! There is no hiding place, for God
Himself took time to build, then sent His Son to
fulfil His Will.

Yes, that Will was done, and as many who believed He called them
Sons and Daughters too. So, what about you? I told you, I slip and
slide, but when you call out – Do you think Jesus run and hide?
His arms swing open, He bids you come. Then all I say
"Thy will be done".

As I was inspired to write this poem, I began to think – Boy! This is a tall order. I wrote this poem a few years after I got saved, or to put it plainly, when I was born again, accepting Jesus as my Saviour and Redeemer.

To be a model requires training and to follow specific instructions. Now as a model for Jesus, a great change began in my new life with new commitment, faith, love, obedience, determination and courage regardless of what came my way. I can honestly tell you that many trials have come my way, but through the mercies of God, I must continue to be that model.

As a model for Jesus I have to rely on the teachings of the Holy Spirit and follow his instructions, and read the Scripture, the Holy Word of God. As a model for Jesus I cannot walk up and down as I like. My steps must be directed by the Lord. I must keep in mind that other people are watching. For many years I lived with my old lifestyle; I walked as I liked, I behaved as I liked, and I lived the way I thought was best for me.

I hope as someone reads this poem, they will see how a new change needs to take place in our lives; old things have to be put away and a new commitment takes it place. I often think of Jesus, when He was on earth walking those dusty roads, with just a pair of sandals. Now He has given me a better pair of shoes, and lots of them. He knows the journey I have to take, and provides me with all I need for this journey.

A MODEL FOR JESUS

A Model for Jesus. People! Come and see.
Dressed in brand new garments
That purchase was a great fee.
So as I walk up and down
Let the light shine out of me.

A Model for Jesus, new shoes too,
I must wear. Just think that He had some
Sandals but he gave me a better pair
"I wonder why".

My roads are rough and stony
Broken glass and sharp edged stones
See! He walked this road before me
He knew my feet must be secure.

A Model for Jesus, a new hat I have
to wear.
My head must be protected,
I can't trust to leave it bare. It is
Such a tender part you see! All nerves
Connected there, so thank you Jesus
For this helmet. I will wear it
Without doubt or fear.

A Model for Jesus, with something in my hand
I just can't flop them by my side.
With no defense, then woe betide.
I tried some gloves but this won't do
So soft there is no strength.
Then Jesus kindly said to me
"Take my staff my child, this cannot bend".

A Model for Jesus, do you know
I wear a breast plate too!
Sometimes the darts are thrown
But somehow they never get through.
So I keep on modeling for Jesus.
A new walk I had to learn.
A new smile too is important
And even how I turn.

So with my new garment, breast plate,
Hat, shoes, staff and his armour too,
I keep on this narrow road
Dare I say it is not an easy walk but
He promised me a safe abode.

My daughter, Lorna, and her husband, Errol, were expecting their third child. They already had two boys, Warren and Julian. How I hoped and prayed that God would give them a little girl. I even made plans to go to help look after the other children when the baby was born. So I travelled down to London once more. In the early hours of the following morning Lorna went into labour and was taken to the Royal Free Hospital.

Now I was still doing some serious praying in my mind as I got the lads ready for school, although they were very independent and dressed themselves for their dad to take them to school before going back to the hospital.

I was now on my own with all sorts going on in my mind. Then the 'phone rang. I answered and this was Errol telling that Lorna had the baby and that it was a boy. I was totally shocked. I found myself saying "Oh dear"! Then I quickly thought - "it's not very nice saying "Oh dear." I said, "That's nice" for I did not want Errol to be hurt by me saying the wrong thing. But, do you know, God had a word for me, and just as I put the 'phone down, I knew I was wrong, for the main thing was that Lorna had delivered safely, and the baby was fine. I was then inspired to write the poem 'Thanksgiving'.

My grandson, Miles Joel, was born on 25 June 1991. He is really lovely and I wouldn't change him now, even if I could, because he is God's own plan.

THANKSGIVING

Dear Lord Jesus, I thank you today,
For I know you heard my call
And answered in your own special way.
This may not be the choice I like
But Lord, who am I to give you advice.
Now with humble heart, I give you praise.
And this I will do always
For high or low, near or far, rich or poor.
You are God over all.

Thank you Lord.

I must say thanks to my sister, Dorcas, who has really encouraged me, and who has typed and put together many of these poems, although not knowing what lies behind any of them. She always says, "God has a purpose for everything".

We both went to Paris to visit my daughter, Elaine. We were in this beautiful park, admiring the flowers, and the children so nicely dressed passing through. The birds and many other things caught our eyes and suddenly I was inspired to write.

We sat on a bench and I took out my pen and paper and began to write about God's Creation. At that time, Dorcas was very quiet, as if she was meditating. Then just as I had finished writing, I said to her "Something strange has happened to me", for I just felt to write as these words came to me".

She then said to me, "Do you believe that I was just thinking of God's creation of the birds, how they are fed and so on. Then I showed her what I had written, entitled 'God's Creation'.

We came home just praising and giving God thanks. We both had a wonderful time in Paris and have visited some lovely places.

GOD'S CREATION

God's Creation – Oh what cheer! Even people in the park,
they do stop and stare.
The flowers, the trees, the leaves swerve with the breeze.
The shrubs that grow, Lord! I know You care for us below.

The children who play and the birds too, they have their ways,
for they need to survive,
while on us they owe their lives.
The faces – some filled with despair,
some with hate.
And some find it hard to understand that we are all the Creation
of God's plan.

Lord help us to give You thanks, for we really look in
Your hands for food and shelter
And raiment too.
But sweet Jesus, it's so nice to know about
You.

Lord, my prayer today is that as men go on their way
And mothers and babies, that in the quietness of their mind
They will hear that still small voice, saying
Jesus loves us, just as we are – Even in the park!

There have been stages in my life when I have looked back and from my heart I can say God has been good to me.

God has blessed me and given me the privilege of travelling to many different countries of the world. One of the most memorable places I visited was Cuba, because it was so tranquil.

My daughter was living in Cuba at that time and took me sightseeing. This was a holiday to remember. I also think of the kindness and the humble nature of the people I got to know and became friendly with. My mind rested as I heard the birds chirping their songs. I saw beautiful gardens, lovely flowers and there was an air of peace surrounding me.

In the calm and quietness, I was inspired to write several poems, which I will share with you. I hope you will feel blessed as you read them.

CUBA - Love

Love can never be measured in tons, metres or pounds,
for true love has no bounds.
Love is like the ocean, it is deep and it is wide, the length
who can reach?
We try so hard to understand.
Why not trust the Maker's Plan.
Love is ever reaching out to one and all,
it brings a message every day in a smile,
in a tear or in a call.
Love is calm, love is peace, love is joy,
which brings tears from the heart to the eyes which cannot
be disguised.
Love has eyes.
Love helps, love kneels, love bows.
Love sends a sweet fragrance which travels around.
Love is meek and yet so strong, it can bring low the mighty man.
Love is pure, yes love is gentle. Oh such peace,
I feel covered in His mantle.

CUBA - Tranquil Moments

Yes, there is peace; Yes, there is calm
I felt the love of God embracing me
I felt secure in His arms.
I felt the Holy Spirit as He quickens
My spirit. O I feel so humble and yet
So confident that whatever happens
His word is my command.
Trust and fear no harm.
As I listened there was such a peace,
As the birds sing their songs I wondered,
Are they saying "Come to the feast"?
Branches are swaying by the strength
Of the wind and such beautiful flowers.
I say thank you to the Creator who makes everything
To Bring Him the glory,
Oh that man would praise Him.

CUBA - Days in the Valley

Days so deep in the Valley only my inward thoughts and me.
Days so deep in the Valley, no one else I see. The path seems long.

Then I thought someone else has passed this way long before me.
"Just carry on, in every Valley God has a plan."

Patience is found in the Valley, I need to understand.

Trust is found in the Valley when there is no one else around,
seen in the midst
God's presence will be found.

Hope is found in the Valley, to take you up the hill.

Strength is found in the Valley, to take you to the mountain.

Courage is found in the Valley, your journey to complete.

So be still in the Valley, for you're never on your own,
your journey to complete.

My last inspiration in CUBA – Perfect Whisper

Such perfect whisper is heard in the wind
Be still, be calm, there will be no harm
Sheltered by the Everlasting Arm,
No need to be alarm.
Such wonderful sounds as the birds
Sing their songs. I could listen to
Their melody all the day long.
Each sings different tunes as mother
Gently makes their nests, to secure their
Young from the heat and distress.
I hear the wind in all its strength
As it gushes through the trees,
Each branch sways from side to side
Then meet together as if to offer
Thanks and praise.
They seem to sway with moving
Rhythm, they bow so low, and
Then so high, then straightens
Up as if they are pointing to the sky.
All things praise Thee Lord Most High.

I was inspired to write this poem while I was staying at my daughter, Lorna, and her husband, Errol's home in London. This was the saddest day of my life, for my youngest daughter Hannah Marie (age 21) died in the tragedy of the Marchioness Disaster on the River Thames in August 1989.

The pain grew harder each day, as Hannah's body was not yet recovered from the water. Not knowing how long this could be was unbearable.

In my distress of heart, the words from Psalm 90:9 came to me: "For all our days are passed away in thy wrath: we spend our years as a tale that is told".

I felt that in spirit that I needed to write these words and I did.

I returned to Nottingham that same evening, and not very long after, I received a call that Hannah's body was recovered from the water. This has been a very painful journey for our family and her friends, for she was greatly loved by all who knew her. I wrote this poem, a Tale That is Told, which I read at her funeral.

I know that life on earth has ended for her, but I am left with precious memories, which I shall cherish forever, until I myself am called Home. I trust that others will find some comfort in the words of this poem, and to know how true it is that our life is Like a Tale That is Told.

A TALE THAT IS TOLD

Yes! Your years are gone as a tale that is told
Most true there is no time to get old
So much to do, loving people, this was your main view
Sharing and caring, my child this was part of you.

A child of promise, such lovely thoughts
The things you said brought joy to our hearts
At times there was pain and trials too, but my
Child, how much we love you.

You spoke of that book, one day we'll write
You started to write, so sorry you lost the fight
But the words live on, and on them I'll stand
For I'm holding on to someone, He alone understands.
So I will keep on writing, I'm sure you want me to
For you were that child of today – Tomorrow I guess
You know there were such pain and sorrow.

So take your rest, Gentle Jesus knows best.
We talked so much about Him
He promised He would help me to stand the test.
I miss your calls and poems too.
Remember you said "Call me by name".
Well that won't be the same.
Child, you never worried, you never complained,
just to see each morning was a great gain,
so happy you were, like the morning rain.
One thing, I'll keep on praying, most sure,
you want me to, and always invite others for I know
Sweet Heaven is in view

Rest in peace.

My daughter, Hannah, also wrote many poems. One day before her death, we were sharing our thoughts as we usually did. She said to me, "Mother, you never know, one day we may write a book together". I'd promised that whenever I put a book together, thoughts about her would be included.

No one truly knows the pain that takes place in an individual's heart when you lose a loved one. I struggle inwardly thinking of the pain she must have felt as she screamed for help that no one was able to give. I often think there were minutes spent calling for mum or "mamsie" as she often called me. But deep down in my heart I also believe she would be calling out to Jesus, for she knew the Lord. Knowing the compassion of Jesus, this gives me hope for Romans 10:13 reads "For whoever shall call upon the name of the Lord shall be saved".

There is no easy way of getting over the death of loved ones, for each person deals with things differently. This I can truly say, knowing Jesus makes all the difference.

I trust this poem "Your last call: Help!" will comfort some, to know that death is not the end.

YOUR LAST CALL: HELP!

Your call for help no one could understand
In desperate moments we all need a helping hand
But strange enough
This last discussion is just between you and God
For He is the One who truly understands.

This cry for help can be heard loud and it reaches far
Like an echo it resounds in my ear
Still this cry can be soft and sweet
As God holds your hand
And you gently kneel at his feet.

This cry for help will lead us home
We get so tired but never alone
Look! That hand that descends
Will take us up and lead us home
He knows the way and our abode
Where, no more endless groans and earthly cries are heard
Only praises, for our child has come home.

Poems by Hannah Marie Harris,
aged 21, who lost her life in the
Marchioness Disaster on the
River Thames on
20th August 1989.

FOR ALWAYS THE SUN SHALL SHINE

For always the sun shall shine upon you. You shall be blessed for
your troubles all the days
of your life, you will be in my presence. I will follow
where you lead, I will sing my praises unto you always.

I will tend to your every fear; whenever you call, I shall be there.

I owe so much – yet how shall I pay – I have
nothing in this world of material attainment – only my heart and
Soul are untouched.

Only these have I to offer for the forgotten misery, for the forgotten
pain. I must never forget my friend, for I owe much more than any
man could gain.

As I rise each morning I pray that
You will grant me just one more day, each day my prayers are
answered.

My mind is intrigued, for what is this force, that leads me to search
deeper, my soul comforts me for there is no mystery in heaven.

You are never ending, each step I take you walk before me with
arms outstretched to cushion me should I fall; only you know my
troubles, only you know my happiness. Though this world keeps
spinning it is standing still, the people are running, scared. They
are running with money, they fail to see for they have closed their
eyes; they do not
know what lies before them for they are too scared to look.

You suggest I should teach them yet what shall I say, Oh Lord give
me the strength to show them the way.
I believe in the birds. I believe in the trees
So why has man closed the door on all these?

BUT I DON'T KNOW HIS NAME

Those cries in the night for that peace out of sight
no longer remain nor does the shame -
of wanting to much, enjoying life -
you must feel the strife but the one within will cleanse all
your sins, make you feel whole, put peace in your soul.

I have not reached my destination but I know
now what direction I must go in.
My feet guide me, but who guides my feet -
no, not my conscious alone for only danger would I meet.

Led by a feeling inside that once He lived and
died to cleanse my soul and make me whole.
He keeps me and you; a teacher through and through.
Asking for little except faith, love and trust.
So small a price to pay to one so righteous.

My life has just begun, but Oh,
what a beautiful song, that has always been sung within me.

Myself – I know who's controlling my destiny
but right now it doesn't fit into my reality,
but that days are coming soon and when it
does, my world and yours will be filled with eternal love!

NEW OR OLD?

Everything seems so new,
so many things happening, I feel quite confused -
what an interesting mixture,
don't feel like a permanent fixture,
too frightened to immense myself in this uncertainty,
as a child I was taught about security.

Dissolutionment reigns, satisfaction disappeared with the passion,
no more artificial lights to illuminate my skies
alone without you, teach me how to survive, without affection,
devotion,
thought I'd be all right – didn't realise how much we had.

This palpitating in my head,
won't let me sleep when I lie in that bed,
I embrace your presence when I remove the fear of being alone,
Listen to some music and then get stoned,
so man, people, birth, life, death,
too many gone without ever knowing that feeling of being loved
to be appreciated, I had it all and decided I as above it!
Seeing the others so fragile, no knowledge of the self-destruction
that they themselves have prepared.

FEELINGS INSIDE

Feel me, watch me, touch me,
I'm here in total harmony,
peace surrounds me,
I'm happy to be here,
never wishing for more than what I had before.
They think I'm tough, never realisiing, how much
my heart too can ache.
I can love you as nobody before,
I can hate you, or simply close the door,
I am capable of feeling all the emotions you feel.

You see everything and nothing,
looking into the future,
Reminiscing about the things that could have been,
you only know the past, don't actually know what's happening now -
with your vague memories, wanting so much, never realsing that
you've already got what you once wished for,
unaware with your memories, can only see the tragedies,
too many people like you in the world,
you've got to learn to accept now.
Only after acceptance comes peace of mind!
Reach out for inner truth, it's inside you.

WHO'S CREATION

God's creation, what a beautiful nation?

Blown by the winds of mystery into
abandonment - imagine the excitement,
never realising at that time
just how much my life was out of line.

Remember the occasions wishing I could tell them,
just how much I cared – always wanted to follow,
but they were too scared. Couldn't show their
feelings, whilst inside voices in my conscious
screaming - "look after him", make sure she gets
this. But who's to maintain my sanity"
Forgotten about in the tragedy.

THE HUMAN RAT RACE

Sanctify me, if you can,
catch me I'm slipping – sipping your wine
forgotten about me in your clash for the line,
sorry wasn't thinking, well about you anyway,
caught up in the acquisitions that always seems to fly my way,
just wanted to tell you, couldn't hold it in for one more day.

They made him a box to pay for his sins,
Mike shouldn't burp it could lead to other things.
Tried to think of how trivial their lives must be
the difference astounding, couldn't see that far behind me.

Them going forward with their two steps back
You'll never fit in my world dear you're black!
I'd better think their way or they'll get me the sack!
Sack, sinking, sank into my twirling chair,
hey I'm cool I haven't got a care,
but suggest that you're otherwise and they'll all be there,
with their questioning eyes, filled with their lies,
they'll never know the difference, quick girl where's your disguise,
of course they know me,
everyone knows me. The girl with the smile and the
energy for a while, until it's gone.
Am I one of them?

I am one of them; yes you're one of us,
we don't even recognise the fact that you're black,
but you slip up baby and they'll get you the sack,
put you back in your place running with the rest
of the blacks in this human rat race!

THE OBSERVER

Watch me, watching you,
but you're too busy with your fleeting emotions,
can't slow down for even a second,
dramatising my life, twisting the knife,
I need to get out now – to escape this man made prison.

Seasons came and went away,
without knowledge of my secret pains,
tears tumble, fears stumble,
can't see the light at the end of the tunnel,
which way now? Your way – says the voice inside me,
keep getting caught in the traps they set out for me,
try to be consistent,
but there are other voices in the distance,
so powerful in their persistence,
waiting for that fatal mistake -
but I see now what route I want to take,
and yes I acknowledge my mistakes.

FLOWERING IN YOUR HAND

Watch me flowering in your hands
Don't say a word, I know you can't understand.
The tears that fall steadily from your searching eyes will secure
A place for you in the skies where no sorrow exists,
a place controlled only by a perfectionist.

No space for the clouds that dulled our skies,
no more darkness to envelop our skies;
no more treachery or lies shall we meet,
only good feelings shall the people receive;
where crowds upon crowds flock to see your face, total
openness I feel no disgrace.

So please! Don't think it's a waste. Not wasting my time
waiting in line,
when my bells ring I'll be up there quick time.
Not wasting my time – I have already seen the sign, and Yes!
I am prepared all of the time.

PEACE

Laugh, be yourself you're with me.

Acknowledge my presence without ambivalence,
visualise if you can the magical sensations that
lie in your hands.

Your mind will withstand the pain,
allow your inner self to expand,
your soul revitalised, crushed the pain
that once had reigned,
the little waves will roll again,
flow back to the source from whence they came.

End of Hannah Marie Harris' poems

MEMORIES

I was 16 when my mother brought this beautiful baby girl home from the hospital. This memory of Hannah has stayed with me and is a constant reminder of how fragile life is.
Lorna

Remembering your cheerfulness; and your call on my birthday December 27th Saying " we December babies need to get together", and we met at our parents house.
Kenneth

21 years have already passed, you're smile is still with me, you're positive attitude keeps me going. I am left with good memories. I miss you very much
Love from sister Elaine

Hannah was a gregarious and loving sister that meant the world to me. She lived every day as though it was her last and never held grudges. She epitomized what being young and carefree was all about.
Chris

Growing up Hannah was always my younger sister, but as she grew out of her teens I remember thinking how the gap narrowed between us, and we could share so much more emotionally and socially. Whenever I see a young black woman around the age of 21, I always think of her.
Chip

You were my favorite daughter. I will never forget the apple pies you always made for me and your out spoken and strong beliefs. The thought of you will live for ever.
Dad

Hannah was a ray of sunshine!! She was bubbly, bright and beautiful. She was incredibly positive, who always saw the good in everything and everyone. Her beauty shone deep! If ever there was anyone to learn from about what it means to be non-judgmental and accepting of others, then it was Hannah
Gloria

MY GUIDE
My guide is the quiet guide, she sends me the right way down darken roads.
Pointing out all life's footfalls and entrapments.
There to lead and me to follow
My light, my guide
John

Hannah was born on Christmas day and was always a guiding light throughout my childhood and teenage years. Whether Hannah was helping me to explore a new opportunity, neighbourhood or experience, her patience and wisdom were always on offer.
Andrew

In this book of poems there are also short inspirations. 'Knowing Jesus' is just one of them that transformed my life. Knowing Jesus has given me hope, a reason for living, a feeling of belonging and a sense of security.

Many people are asking "What has gone wrong"? I think of the many things that have gone wrong in the world today: drug addiction, thefts, loss of respect, ungodliness, drunkenness, suicide, and these are just a few.

Some people today seem to have no time to stop for a moment even to think of the love of Jesus, and to give thanks for a new day. Many believe that whatever they achieve in life it's their hard work that got them there. Jesus has nothing to do with it. How sad! In saying all of this, I do not mean that knowing Jesus excludes us from the problems and difficulties of life, trials of different sorts and persecution. However, we face these problems and move on with our daily lives.

The beauty of all this is that in times of our trials we know who to call upon, we can stand upon His words. In 2 Peter 5:7 (Kings James Version) says "Casting all your cares upon Him for he careth for you". His words are true.

I have experienced Jesus in my own life, this is why I can write these words, which I was inspired to do. I will continue to trust Him still, in times of trials because I know Jesus never fails. I can rest upon His word.

I trust that in the words from this short verse, you will receive the assurance that even in the darkness you may know Jesus will be with you.

KNOWING JESUS

Knowing Jesus makes the difference in this changing world below
In the darkness He will be with you, and the light will show.
Be still He faileth never, and rest upon His word
even when tempted to question
Just trust God and be bold.

Two years after the death of my daughter, Hannah, in 1989, there was still much sadness in my heart. The memory of her death; the constant reminders, especially when I attend funerals, and the funny things we laughed and talked about comes flooding back to me.

In the company of friends I feel that I can cope with the internal pain, but as the words of his poem says "At times my heart grew sad and lonely, no one in sight I see, all I can do is shut the door and know I am alone with thee". This makes me think of my favourite hymn – 'Never Alone'.

I thank God for faithful friends, who in their spare moments lend their ears and bend their knees in humble acknowledgement to my family and me.

I was inspired to write this poem knowing that God is holding me with his hands. This poem speaks of the "tears that ran down my face like droplets of rain". How true!

So I thank you Lord for everything, my joys and my pains. Let me with thankful heart forever keep listening to your Word, for one day I will hear you say – Welcome Home.

HE HELD ME WITH HIS HANDS

He held me by my hands! I held on to his Words.
In times when all was silent, great wonders were unfolded as he said,
"Be still and know that I am God and truly God alone".
At times my heart grew sad and lonely, no one in sight I see
I just shut the doors and made to know I am alone with Thee.

Sometimes I feel on mountains high what joys overflow my soul,
If I but have the wings of a dove no more this world I would roam.
But true enough from mountain's top He brings me down to earth
and said my child in me abide,
I am your God and guide, and then what can I ask besides?

Some times in valleys Oh! So dark great shadows cover me,
But true enough his guiding hands have always reached down for me,
And when I think I am alone, He tells me I am with thee.
My tears ran down, like drops of rain, so warm upon my face,
But truly I cannot store them, or else they would fill this place.

But there again my Saviour said "My child just trust in grace,
This is sufficient it will fill this place".

So thank you Lord, for everything; my joys, my pains,
And even fears, for out of them you lead me, you guide my weary days.

I thank you Lord for faithful friends, in lonely hours an ear they lend,
and knees that bow and humbly pray. Father guide your children
on our way.
So with thankful heart I will keep on listening.
One day as my Lord says "My child, well done.
Into my Kingdom come".

I give thanks for this poem 'Guiding Light'. We live in a world where everything to the natural eye looks wonderful and bright. The light that shines from Jesus has a special glow.

The pleasures of life and the beauty of things that surround us can dim our vision from following this guiding light. In this life we are all on a journey, and, as we humbly go up hills; down valleys; through deserts and snow; and through bends of life that we cannot see – that guiding path my Saviour shows.

On the hills you can have a good view of places far away, and enjoy the beauty of God's creation. In the valley one can feel closed in, and caused to look up; for the climb back to the top can be very hard. This calls for perseverance and humility.

The desert experience can be scary; everything around looks dry and you become thirsty. In the desert, we learn to appreciate the many things we take for granted. In the desert, our hearts are opened to reason. In the desert, our hope can be strengthened or we can feel deflated.

When we surrender our will to the Saviour, we will be guided by His light that will shine through us. Then we can go through the bends of life that we cannot see. Soon others will see there is a difference in us and they too will want to know about the Saviour.

This journey is not always easy. Still, we have the promise of God which stands sure. Let us keep in mind that this journey was not easy for Jesus, yet He trusted His Father and endured the cross so He could be our Guiding Light.

MY GUIDING LIGHT

You are my star and guiding light
No other light I know.
No light in this world to compare with Your glow
To guide us on our journey as we go.
This light shines on, as we humbly go through
Hills, valleys, desert and snow.
Through bends of life that we cannot see.
That guiding path my Saviour shows.

Sometimes in the valley so deep beneath,
No way to climb back to the site -
But do you know; He is the Way.
Give Him your hand without delay.
This light must shine in this world below,
For others to follow, the Saviour they should know.
Come, see we are all travelling to that City,
Where brighter lights do shine, where our
Saviour awaits us as we hand in our lights.

There is a place called Glory
My friends, I will meet you there.
For my Saviour is gone before me,
And His Glory lingers near.
Thank you Lord

The words of this poem have encouraged me to hold on to God's promises whatever life throws at me. I have experienced both the rough and the smooth in my life; this is why I can share my testimonies with others. There were times when I felt like giving up or even running away, but deep within me there was something holding me and keeping me strong within.

I knew that I could not endure the many trials I faced alone. I give thanks for the Brethrens of my Church, and truly they were my support. I needed their help, holding up my hands in prayer, also their encouraging words, for we are called to bear each other's burdens. If I falter from following through, my witness would be worthless, and my life is in vain.

One has to be disciplined in many ways when called to be a witness. We have to face people whose faces are so stern and seem so hard. We are called to be humble, yet confident, for the eyes of people are always watching us. Our lights must shine for others to see the love of God in us.

I take comfort in the words of this poem, which came to be while I was in London visiting my daughter and her husband and the grandchildren. This is a home where I always enjoy a great peace. Over the years I have seen many changes, but I am so thankful that God never change. By His Grace, I am determined to hold on.

HOLD ON

If I let go, "What have I got to show"?
How could others know if I let go?
So get to the Church and fall in line,
They are the support, so don't waste time.
Go bring them in, for there are souls to win,
The Saviour is waiting, this work must begin.
Don't let go for the Saviour will want to know.
Where is the trust He left us, "Where did it go"?

There is a lot to conquer, so do not be afraid.
For hard faces too; Lord I am trusting you for
Your love can re-arrange. We can be malleable,
And yet be strong, you know the Saviour is always
Willing to give a helping hand. You can be humble
And yet confident, so don't give in for with the
Saviour we must win. So take my command and stand arm in arm.
The Saviour will guide you, He makes the demand.
We are his soldiers, together we stand,
For He will guide us, to that blessed Promised Land.

Thank you Lord.

Tuareg Productions LTD

Brighter Days is published by
Tuareg Productions Ltd

C/O Citycas Ltd, Suite 540, Fifth Floor,
Linen Hall, 162-168 Regent Street, London W1B 5TP.

Email: press@tuaregproductions.com
www.tuaregproductions.com
Tel: 0207 692 2711

Print & Design provided by
Contract Publishing UK

Email: enquiries@contractpublishinguk.co.uk
Website: www.contractpublishinguk.co.uk
Telephone: +44(0)1480 861 962